Copyrights

No part of this book may be reproduced or transmitted in any form or by any means, electronic or mechanical, including photocopying, recording, or by any information storage and retrieval system, without permission in writing from the copyright owner.

The right of **Bill Allerton** to be identified as the author of this work has been asserted by him in accordance with the Copyright, Designs and Patents Act, 1988.

Most characters in this publication are fictitious and any resemblance to real persons, living or dead, is purely coincidental.

Where real or recognisable historical characters are featured, they are used in an entirely fictional capacity with no intent to demean or subvert their image or memory.

Text:	© Bill Allerton 2025
Cover & Graphics:	© Cybermouse Books 2025
Typeset & Layout:	© Cybermouse Books 2025
Font:	Garamond 12pt.

ISBN: 978-1-0686097-8-7

Cybermouse Books
90 St. Anthony Rd.
Sheffield S10 1SG
www.cybermouse.co.uk

Published by Cybermouse Books 2025

In the design of this book, Cybermouse Books have made every effort to avoid infringement of any established copyright.
If anyone has valid concern re any unintended infringement please contact us first at the above address.

Cover Image: © Chatgpt and Me

All rights reserved.

NEARER MY GOD

a
Novella

by

Bill Allerton

THE PROLOGUE:

is an exercise in summation in one sentence…

THE NOVELLA:

is dedicated to those who only dream of life, instead of grasping the heart of it in both hands and allowing themselves to live it while awake…

Bill Allerton

PROLOGUE:

Imagine a small town, enfolding small people living small lives while it cleaves to the ground on which it sits by the fingernails of those who exist within its sounds, yet, within the smallness of the sounds those small people make there are great people hidden deep, whose great lives are often stymied by the sweltering cocoon of small friendships while through them run unseen rivers of hope and wish that pour torrential and unheard beneath the streets and practices of it just being a small town drowning in the rattle of its own automobiles, the barking of its dogs and the chatter of passing children, the scrape of shoes on its sidewalks, its shop-front glass of shattering illusions and the scents of sugar candy, coffee and spent gasoline riding the air that all of its people, small and great alike, breathe in and expel, each placing their own immortal marker in another's breath while partaking what they will of the breath of all the souls that ever lived and prospered in small towns such as this and here it waits, hanging by a fingernail, suffocated by time, continually replicating people to walk its streets, eat in its cafés or stare in admiration or despair at this microcosm they have been created to house their wisdom, or lack thereof, while standing in awe of those who attempt to open their small lives to greatness with tall and wondrous dreams of love, happiness and adventure but, most of all, with a curiosity for what lies beyond the narrow confines of horizons peculiar only to themselves, set to be held or broached at will and tempered by the need to touch and measure the dimensions of others who also walk these same automobile-ridden, town-scented, clattering, spectrally-rivered streets, hearing clearly the bright contentions of the children they had forgotten they ever were.

NEARER MY GOD

Guiseppe Marino wakes with a start, struck by a notion that in all his seventy-eight years he can't remember ever having travelled by airplane.

He tracks his sleep for the fading tendrils of the dream then climbs from his bed to shake the day through his mind and limbs. His image stands tall in the mirror, golden-tipped of hair, eyes so clear and dark you could sail a dream in them, but that is just a wished-for reflection that he knows will never return.

He will ring Maurice after breakfast, after shaving, after finding a clean-ish shirt amongst the pile on the floor and after doing the best he can to make himself feel like a vague shadow of the man in the mirror.

*

The voice of Maurίce Gonzalez drizzles like cold syrup from the phone.

'Hey… Seppy?'

'You asleep, Maurίce?'

'Was.'

Guiseppe is silent for a moment, his mind still searching for the notions of that dream. He holds the phone away from his face to stare down into the earpiece. His thoughts filter through the tiny holes and into Maurίce's darkened bedroom to that little blackened side-table where Maurίce keeps his phone and his pills, waiting for a sunrise that never quite makes it through the thick, brown curtains Nella left behind.

He takes a breath, imagining he can smell Maurice's apartment as the decaying remains of a living thing, one that has hidden itself away from the burn of daylight as might a wounded animal.

There had only ever been one light in that place. One thankfully never connected to Maurice's spurious wiring, but bearing a light all of its own.

Until God had unplugged it.

*

Maurice slides out of bed and straight into his slippers.

There are no mirrors in his room. He doesn't need a mirror to know that he is just as old, bent and raddled as the man on the other end of the telephone.

Maurice waits him out. Then gives in, just to fill the void developing between them.

'Coffee, Seppy?'

'Okay.'

'Downstairs?'

'Fine, but tell…'

'Don't worry, Seppy. I got this.'

Maurice puts down the telephone and makes his way around the bed. He stands in front of the window, gripping a curtain in each hand and closes his eyes against impending daylight.

With a sudden bravado he whips the curtains back and daylight falls around him like the rush of a clear river, cloaking him in a luminescent shroud woven from the world outside. It streams on into the room, seeking diversion amongst old, dark furniture and the faded paper violets that climb the walls, jarring their brighter hues where portraits of previous tenants had once hung. It plays amongst the filtered crumple of ancient bed linens until they seem a thing of shame, of an unsterile sterility that once seen, will now need to be changed.

Behind the light comes the noise from the street below that Nella's curtains had silenced... chairs scraping across wine-stain sidewalks, spoons lost to the harsh floor in a bright jangle, the bark of motor car horns, footsteps, and the high-pitched chirrup of children escaping the enforced quiet of a schoolroom just because it is a Saturday.

He opens the window wide and air follows the sound into the room, but the light has already caused so much damage that he knows its added effect will remain insignificant.

Down below Maurice's window is a faded awning striped in orange, lemon and white. He takes off a slipper and throws it onto the top of the awning, where it sits like a boat on sun-slivered water.

From under the canvas, the end of a broom handle knocks it back into the air. As it falls from the edge it is caught and then expertly thrown back up and through Maurice's window. He steps aside to let it pass.

A woman's voice shouts from below, her enquiring eyes peering up at him from beneath a fat, round bob of curled black hair.

'Usual, Maurice?'

Maurice shakes his head and holds up two fingers.

'That all, Maurice?'

He shakes his head again and folds one of the fingers in half.

With a nod of, 'Okay.' Oroteña disappears back under the awning.

*

'I'm comfortable here, Maurice.' Seppy rocks his chair back onto two legs until, from behind, Oroteña slaps him back onto all four. Seppy's knees catch at the table edge and the cups rattle in their saucers.

Maurice grabs at the table. 'It must be the service, Seppy. It's never this personal anywhere else.'

'All these years since Nella, Maurice. You never looked twice at this woman?'

'She throws too mean a slipper. So what's this all about?'

'I woke up this morning and suddenly I was aware of all the things I haven't done. Places I haven't been.'

'That's some list, Seppy.'

'So I got out of bed and looked in the mirror…'

'Never a good move…'

'…and I thought…'

'Two bad moves in a row, Seppy. A third might be a catastrophe.'

'…I thought that I wanted to taste the air.'

'Still tastes the same. Exhaust fumes, garlic and old farts like you and me. You just got used to it.'

'Not around here, Maurice. Somewhere different to this. Somewhere there may be taste left in the world. Something to savour through the lips… like a good strong coffee... I'm never sure how Oroteña knows how much sugar to put in mine.'

'It's a mystery of life itself, Seppy.'

Oroteña eases her bulk into a chair beside them. 'You boys still got some fat to chew?'

Maurîce takes a look around the café. 'What about your other customers?'

'You mean the ones in each corner buried in their laptops? They scared out everybody else.'

'Serves you right for getting broadband.'

'Accountant said it was good for business.'

'Accountants are never good for business. The year after you go bust they tell you exactly why. To the penny. Less their fee. Take Seppy here... never had a head for business so he never needed an accountant. Take a long look at him.'

'What..?'

'Either look and learn or go get more coffee. You too old to learn?'

'What am I looking at?'

'Just look, woman. Tell me what you see.'

'God, Maurîce. Just about breathing is all he's doing. What's so special about that?'

'He's 78 years old.'

'And..?'

'And all without the aid of an accountant.'

Guiseppe sits up in his chair and grabs at the coffee cup. He drains it to the dregs then licks the unstirred sugar from the bottom with a long, rust-coloured tongue.

'Anybody know a good one?'

Oroteña heaves herself from the chair. 'You heard

all his jokes, Seppy. Times over. I'll get the coffee.'

Guiseppe reaches across to tap Oroteña on the arm. 'No. A good accountant.'

Maurice laughs out loud. 'Why would you of all people want an accountant, Seppy. You been a wage-slave all your life.'

Guiseppe draws his sudden thought back in across the table, retrieving it from Maurice's criticism. His face clouds up and he glances around the café for Oroteña's broad beam making its way back through the scattering tables.

'I've been getting letters, Maurice. They're full of figures that I don't understand.'

Maurice takes the new cups from Oroteña's hands. 'What are you doing with them?'

'I put them in a box under the bed.'

'Sounds expensive, Seppy. I'd burn them. They'll only be tax demands or such. Nobody gives nothing for nobody no time not here.'

Oroteña scribbles a number on her receipt pad. 'Here Seppy. Try this number. He's not cheap and he may be no better than the rest of them… but he's the Devil I know.'

*

Guiseppe smoothes the creases from his least-worst trousers with a careful hand, retrieves the yellow shirt from the bottom of the wardrobe, takes one look at the fly-away collar then throws it back in. However had he not noticed that in the charity shop? Fifty years ago maybe he could have carried that off. He picks it up again, then drops it back. Or maybe never, he thought, before picking it up again.

*

'Señor Marino.'

Carmelo Adagio, the Accountant, has a voice equally as dark as the office panelling surrounding them.

Guiseppe in his bright yellow shirt feels more like a target than a client.

'Guiseppe… please.'

'Señor Marino. There is no easy way to tell you this.'

Guiseppe hitches the chair closer to the desk so he doesn't miss a thing. 'Do you think you could say it in a way that a man like me could understand?'

'Let me start by saying that I have spent many hours going through the box of paperwork you brought me last week. I have spent even more hours chasing financial rabbits down holes that turn out to be either a cul-de-sac or have so many twists and turns they would grace the roller-coaster they drag in for the Fiesta come Saturday.'

'I never was good at figures. Fish I could count, and weigh, and sell. But numbers…'

'Señor Marino… Guiseppe… Is there anyone I can call? You might not wish to be alone… your age, you see.'

Guiseppe stops to think for a moment, recalling Maurice's implied criticism and wondering how many 'I Told You So's' a man can deal with in one lifetime. Oroteña? No. Too close but not close enough, if that makes any sense at all. He searches his memories and comes up with an image of a smile. He folds his complete sense of self-preservation inside the memory of Nella.

'I'll be okay. No news seems so bad after others I can recall.'

'Well. If that's alright with you, Señor… Guiseppe… sit quietly… and we'll be as gentle as we can…'

He touches a button on his desk and a tall, upright man in a dark suit enters the office with the briefest of knuckle raps on the door.

'Señor Marino.' The Accountant paints the stifling air within the office with the depth of his intonation. 'I would like to introduce you to Señor Rallentandó. He is a Solicitor of my long acquaintance who will help you to understand the legacy left to you by your uncle.'

Guiseppe shuffles in the hard chair.

'How much will he charge me?'

Señor Rallentandó extends a hand towards him… and waits… the fingers half-curled in anticipation as they hang in mid-air. He withdraws it slowly and feigns embarrassment.

'The best advice is always the cheapest, Señor Marino. Whatever it may cost.'

Guiseppe sits back until the hard chair rail imprints his shoulder blades.

'My father's best advice was alway to assess your ability to pay before embarking on any venture.'

'Wise words. Wise words indeed!' The solicitor leans forward into his revelation. He has wanted to present this news to Guiseppe for days, since first having heard of it. He will dine out on this one for months to come. 'But your father's very much younger brother… was the lucky one.'

Guiseppe scowled at him.

'I heard that he died alone and lonely. Is that what you would call lucky?'

'I meant financially lucky, of course, and sometimes one circumstance precludes the other.'

'So you wish to transfer his curse onto me, now? I have no wish to die alone, even though we all must, I suppose.'

The solicitor stares hard at the wall opposite, watching his fee slide slowly down the darkly-grained surface.

'Señor Marino, we are here today to offer you the option to take the reward of your uncle's windfall legacy or to walk away, even though that would be inadvisable, both personally and legally.'

'Why would that be?'

'My dear sir, 'Affairs' are meant to be tied up, assigned, stamped, sealed and filed as having been dealt with in the gravest and most legal of manners.'

'He couldn't have taken it with him?'

'Señor Marino… there is a subtle irony in that expression because on your Uncle's last flight from this life he would have had no need of the legacy.'

Guiseppe takes a sudden interest in the conversation. He leans slightly forward.

'Why not?'

'Because…' Señor Rallentandó's hope for a fee drags itself up from the carpet and begins to climb. He leans in towards Guiseppe. '…the Angels make no charge.'

*

Oroteña looks around, past Guiseppe and over his shoulder.

'No Maurice?'

'That's right.' Guiseppe puts both hands flat upon the table. 'No Maurice. Not this time.'

Oroteña pulls out a chair.

'That's like Cain without Abel. You're much more fun when you're killing each other.'

Guiseppe turns his hands palms up. 'Sit down.'

'Hey! This is my café… remember?'

Guiseppe drops his hands into his lap where the fingers twine like lianas around a mangrove.

'Please.'

'That's better.'

Oroteña sits beside him. It is inevitable that parts of her make contact with Seppy along one side as she leans into him but he is uncertain about the level of intimacy that follows the movement of heat from her loins into his.

He experiences a sudden urge to move away, to put some small distance between himself and the flesh he is aware is held tightly from him by a mere frailty of summer cloth. But the wall is in the way. She leans further into him, her great weight blossoming over the chair seat.

'Oroteña… you don't mind I call you Oroteña?'

'Of course not, Guiseppe. But just in case you might think that I am thinking that you are thinking that we might be thinking… together. You know?'

'Oh no… Heaven forfend.'

'That's alright. Then it's only polite to use my full

name amongst friends. As a child I was always called Big O.'

'Oh… but kindly, I assume? I mean…'

'What rock do you live under, Seppy? You ever know anyone around here to be kind?'

'You are always kind… to me anyway.'

'That's nothing that a slap around the head wouldn't cure. Coffee, Seppy? Or are you waiting for Maurice?'

'I can't find him.'

'He was down the corner placing a bet, earlier.'

'I never placed a bet, Oroteña. Does he win?'

'If he comes back wearing a shirt then he's had a good day. And an even better one for those that have to look at him.'

She turns away to stare at the coffee machine in the corner. 'All those wrinkles.' Her shoulders ripple a tsunami of shudder.

'Guiseppe?'

'Yes, Oroteña?'

'My other name is written over the door.'

'Oh… I never noticed.'

'Thirty years, Guiseppe, so maybe it hasn't had time to sink in yet.'

Guiseppe swallows hard, then fills his lungs with what he thought was to be a sigh but then, with a sudden twist, as she returns to the table with the cups, marks the beginning of a confession.

'I have something to tell you.'

Oroteña looks up to the awning to see that Maurice's slipper has appeared silently above them like an unmoored boat.

'Is this a secret?'

Guiseppe stares into her eyes. To see the hunger in there. To see the thirst for something new and more exciting than coffee and churros and the rearrangement of tables.

He looks up to the slipper riding the printed waves of the awning and knows that it will not stay secret for long.

He gives her the intangible key to it.

'You must not tell Maurice yet. I am not ready for that.'

*

'So what are you going to do about it, Seppy?'

Guiseppe shakes his head in weariness.

'Maurice, I really have no idea.'

'You could leave the country, I suppose.'

'Why would I do that?'

'Why would you not? Seems like everyone knows where to find you.'

'I've never hidden in my life, Maurice. Things, maybe. Feelings, all the time. But never this…'

Seppy strokes his open hands down along his torso in an encompassing gesture. 'Never hid this.'

Maurice leans over and pretends to sniff at him.

'Fish. Takes some hiding.'

Oroteña sways across to the table with three coffees.

'Sorry, Seppy. Bad news travels fast. What are you going to make of it?'

'He doesn't know. I told him he should absent himself from all the trouble it will bring.'

Oroteña pushes a cup across the table. 'Drink your

coffee and shut up, Maurice. He's big enough to make up his own mind. So, Seppy. What's the news?'

'I never been on an airplane.'

'That's not news, Seppy. Losing it?'

'Maurice has. Tell me what it's like, Maurice.'

'Losing it?'

'No. The airplane.'

'Never did.'

'Maurice. Don't lie to me.'

'I'm not lying but, like I said, that's not news.'

'You took Nella to the Bahamas.'

'On a boat, Seppy. On a boat.'

'You said you flew.'

'Only thing flew that vacation was the time. Remember Nella back then?'

And Guiseppe does. He remembers her young and how, in his eyes that had followed her each and every move, she had never changed from the moment he first saw her. She had never shrivelled to dust on the clean, white shelf of her bed as if time itself were being sucked out of her, leaving her at the last with only a smile he will remember forever. However long forever turns out to be. There are days he feels that smile is a burden he ought to put down, along with his bones. Would that he too, in that time, had such a smile.

His lips turn down as his thoughts drift back to Maurice's vacation in the Bahamas. The only thing time did for him then was to drag its feet so heavily across the carpet there is no wonder that now it looks so worn. The tracks from the kitchen to the TV and from there to the bedroom, and especially the one from there to the bathroom, were signs any blind man might follow without a cane.

Guiseppe's throat is clogged and his tongue heavy with unspoken words he has held for two decades.

'Yes.' Is all he can bring himself to say.

There are days when he hates Maurice. He hates him for being his one and only friend. When he needs to bitch about Maurice to someone else is when he feels most truly lost and alone.

Maurice rarely bitches. At least not to him. Not about anything. Anything of which there must be a multitude from which to choose.

'Take your hook out, Maurice.'

'Okay, Oroteña. I'll leave him be. But leave him be what?'

'Whatever he wants. What does he want?'

Guiseppe, hands still on torso, looks around in mock surprise.

'What? Am I invisible all of a sudden that you should talk about me like this?'

'It's the fish, Seppy.'

'Eighteen years, Maurice. Count them…' Guiseppe holds up one hand and trips the fingers of the other across it like a practiced pianist. '…since these last carried a box of fish.'

Maurice wields an invisible rod in the air.

'I know, Seppy, but you still thrash around on my hook like a line-caught tuna.'

Oroteña crushes his hands to the table.

'Leave him be, Maurice. You don't want *I* should reel *you* in.'

*

You could leave the country, I suppose.

Maurice's words play over again like a scratched record inside Guiseppe's head the next morning. He'd woken during the night and there they were, drifting like the news feed on the tv across the bottom edge of his wakefulness.

How on earth could he even start to leave the country, the place that had given him birth then sustained him for seventy-eight years?

The question pursued him through corn mush and milk and yesterday's warmed-over coffee. The only instruction that life had given him was to stay put and make the best of it. In that way, a man could cope with the responsibilities that span out of his own actions. Or lack thereof.

It was a choice, and Life shouldn't thrust things like that upon a man whose choice it had been to remain static.

Perhaps the Church has an answer.

*

Guiseppe had always found Padre Abejundio a little disconcerting. The beatific smile beneath a crisp black birretta seemed barely to hide the bee sting of criticism implied by his name.

'Good morning, Guiseppe. How may I help you today?'

'Good morning, Padre. May we enter the Confessional?'

The Padre makes an elaborate gesture, sweeping

aside the hem of his cassock to expose the threshold into the box.

'Mind the step, Guiseppe. I know this as a place you may have lost the knowledge of.'

'There is nothing wrong with my memory, Padre.'

'The years take a toll, Guiseppe. How many has it been?'

'For one like myself who never sins, it has always seemed a pointless journey.'

'We all carry sin, Guiseppe. Why, this very morning you must have walked through the town to be here.'

'And that is a sin, Padre?'

'As we walk amongst the town, Guiseppe, we breathe the exhalations of murderers, footpads, pederasts and thieves. How can we not participate in their sin when the molecules of their breath lodge deep into a man's heart and from there spread to all parts of his Mortal Soul.

'If that is the case Padre, Sunday Mass after Promenade must be full of sinners. How does one Priest manage?'

'The work is hard, Guiseppe, but it is within my compass to expiate such incipiently guilty breath when and wherever I can.'

'Padre… In the seventy-eight years I have walked God's Earth, surely I must have also inhaled molecules of the living breath exhaled by Christ. Would you expiate that too?'

The Padre leans closely to the mesh separating them. His words pass quietly between the two compartments of the booth.

'Guiseppe? Will you hear my confession?'

*

'Half-a-Million, Seppy! I can't even count that in my head. What are you going to do with it?'

'It's not mine yet, Maurice.'

'So what makes it yours?'

'A decision…'

'So make it, Seppy. Settle the affair and get back to being you again.'

'What was I, Maurice?'

'Well… I guess…'

'Exactly.'

'No, Seppy. I didn't mean it like that. You're not a Zero.'

'Then what am I?'

'As of now?'

'Yes.'

'You're Half-a-Million of Zeros.'

'That's a lot of nothing, Maurice. You can get a lot of zeros in a very small bucket. And what if I don't want to carry the bucket?'

'Well, Seppy… you have friends.'

'I have you and Oroteña. You mean I could buy more?'

'But then they wouldn't be friends, Seppy.'

'Then what are you suggesting?'

'Well… I think we'd be happy to help you out if you ran out of ideas.'

'You didn't think I had any ideas two days ago. So what changed?'

'Two days ago you didn't need any ideas, Seppy.

That's what changed. But you're trying to decide on nothing. You can't do that. Go sign the papers then you'll have something to decide over and maybe then you'll get some ideas.'

'What if I don't want it.'

'Seppy, I no longer care what you do or don't want. In fact I don't care if you burn it all to keep warm next winter. Just do something about it for Christ's sake. Get off my hook!'

*

'What do I need to do?'

Señor Rallentandó pushes a small sheaf of papers across the desk. Guiseppe draws them to him, turns them around and begins to read.

'I don't understand, Señor. What are all these 'wherefores', 'whatsoevers' and 'In Terms Absolute'? But then, 'irrevocable transfers' seems maybe worst of all.'

'Señor Marino, this is merely how I earn my fee.'

Guiseppe shuffles the papers into an orderly pile and hands them back.

'By offering me confusion? I do that for free every morning when I look in the mirror.'

'Guiseppe… may I call you Guiseppe?'

'It's a little formal but okay.'

'Guiseppe. What do you expect to see in the mirror?'

'I don't know. A fading bloom of youth, maybe?'

'Well, as your solicitor, I can assure you that it is still there.'

'When did you become *my* solicitor? And do you

have some special kind of insight? Like the taxman?'

'No, Guiseppe. It's just that solicitors are trained to look beneath the surface of things. We see detail that is buried deep by language and we use that same language to expose the devil that resides there.'

'You mean the one placed there earlier by yet another solicitor?'

'I'm afraid so, Guiseppe. And we also look beneath the surface of a man. We have to, to find out who we can and cannot trust.'

'I thought solicitors trusted no-one?'

'You are that rare thing, Guiseppe. A man whose fading bloom of youth still resides in his detail and requires only that the layers of Life be peeled back to reveal it.'

'Fish, Señor.'

'Fish, Guiseppe?'

'Layers of Fish, Señor.'

'I don't understand.'

'Señor, language is a box of freshly caught fish. Words slip, slide and slither over others in layers, each searching for best place in an ever-changing position and they're all after the same thing.'

'And what might that be, Guiseppe?'

'Oxygen, Señor.'

'Oxygen?'

'Yes. With your breath you inflate each and every word and pressure them into self-importance.'

'Is this what you think solicitors do, Guiseppe?'

'Oh no, Señor. Solicitors just rearrange the fish boxes to benefit their own purpose.'

'And your purpose too, Guiseppe.'

'May I ask you a question, Señor?'

'Of course.'

'If my best purpose is to remain as who, what and where I am at this moment, what will happen to your fee?'

Señor Rallentandó pushes his chair away from the desk and leans back to study the look on Guiseppe's face. Suddenly, even after all his years of practise, he finds that look unreadable.

He stares searchingly down at his own hands folded gently in his lap, looking for a remnant of lost skill, perhaps beneath the nails with which he has clung to this profession for so many years. Finding none, he looks up with a smile and reaches out to draw the papers back toward himself.

Guiseppe's hand slams down upon them before they have moved an inch.

'Show me where I sign.'

'But Guiseppe… I thought…?'

In the flash before the solicitor can rotate the pages, Guiseppe recalls the moment that Nella had told him she had cancer. He had cried so hard until she had spoken to him so gently and finely that he had looked up into her face and found that she was smiling.

'Señor Rallentandó. In the words of someone infinitely wiser than myself, 'Que sera, sera."

'El Testamento de Dios, Guiseppe.'

Guiseppe smiles again, watching the solicitor put pencil 'X's where he is expected to sign.

'But only…Señor… if God is a woman.'

*

'So what was his fee, Seppy?'

'He agreed to take one fifth of the estate.'

'Ouch! I once had a dog with a jaw that size. It's teeth were…'

'It's not a problem, Maurice. It's what I offered him. I shall never be able to use all the rest. Maybe it will do him some good.'

'But a fifth!'

'Maurice! Let it go.'

'That's what I told that dog but it wouldn't until I beat it's brains out with a stick. Shall I go back and try it out on Shylock?'

'Maurice…'

'Okay. So you need a smaller bucket. We can live with that.'

'We?'

'Well… you'll need to have ideas from time to time. I can be your sounding board.'

'And Oroteña?'

'Hmm… Loudspeaker?'

*

'So what does half-a-million in zeros look like, Seppy?'

Guiseppe hands Oroteña a small plastic card. She turns it over and over in her fingers but, apart from an unfamiliar logo in one corner, there's just his name and a string of numbers.

'What is it?'

Guiseppe gently removes it from her hand.

'It's a very small bucket.'
'Can you buy coffee with it?'
'No.'
'Why not?'
'It's Maurice's round.'
'But you have money.'
'And if I paid for everything he would lose his self-respect.'

Oroteña kicks the leg of Maurice's chair so that it settles square on the floor. 'Not that he ever had any.'

Guiseppe slips the card into a slim plastic folder and places it in his inside jacket pocket.

'And anyway…' He glances up at her. 'What makes you think that it's money?'

*

The telephone rings out beside Guiseppe's bed. He slides his feet into the slippers with the broken-down heel and shuffles them gracelessly across the little hall from the kitchen and into the bedroom.

'Hello?'

'Seppy? That you?'

'If you have another life to wait, Maurice, I'll go and check.'

'Seppy? Would you like a coffee? Oroteña would like to talk to you.'

'Only Oroteña?'

'Well… no. I would like to talk too.'

'Is this about money, Maurice? Only I wondered with you phoning me I thought someone must have paid your bill. You come into a fortune?'

'Don't grind, Seppy. I thought we were all friends.'

'And then some. So what do you want, Maurîce, you know, apré coffee?'

'It's a thought about being friends. We want to share in something with you.'

'My good fortune?'

'Yeah, something like that, Seppy. Something like that.'

'How many fish boxes you think you can carry between you, Maurîce?'

'I don't know. How many you got?'

'Seventy eight years worth, give or take. Half sugar in mine.'

Guiseppe lowers the handset slowly into the cradle then lowers himself onto the bed beside it. He checks his battered old wristwatch and strokes again for luck the side of the bezel where the gold plate has long since worn from it. Under his finger shines polished base metal.

He recognises that only too well. It happens when you scratch the surface of any man… and most women. His thoughts rub the surface of his memories of Nella. Still gold. Not all women, then.

He checks again to see if ten minutes has passed. At least six of which he knows Maurîce will have spent fidgeting in his seat and scratching at his arse, his mouth filled with dreams of gold and words of base wisdom bursting yet not daring to overspill until the moment he, Guiseppe, arrives at the table.

From downstairs he hears the hiss of the Gaggia machine on Oroteña's counter.

He listens again and smiles to himself… or that

sound could be coming from Maurice.

He descends the stairs carefully into the café.

*

Oroteña comes to the table with three coffees in saucers, one held between her fingers, two more balanced along a prodigious forearm. With her other hand she draws out a chair, then sets the cups down before crushing her behind into the bright aluminium seat.

On her left is Maurice. To her right is Guiseppe and somehow this feels appropriate. If asked why, she realises there would be no cogent answer. Sometimes these feelings she has transcend explanation. Her mother, *Dios guarde su alma*, had been clairvoyant. Or so she had claimed when in her cups, although Oroteña considered her strike record of under ten percent to be less convincing than pure chance.

Growing up, Oroteña's mother had tried to train her in the 'ways of seeing', but the only future Oroteña had seen was that there was unlikely to be one. Cash was harder. Cash was real. Cash had a promise of fulfilment written across it in ink. Until the government went tits up, anyway. But this had only happened twice in her lifetime. The only correct prediction Oroteña could remember was that her mother had told her one night, in a deep Tequila Trance, that if she didn't stop eating cake she would become fat.

And now, to her left, Maurice is silently working his mouth in a grimace, teeth quietly grinding back the offer they had dreamed up between themselves over a breakfast coffee. His hands are tugging at the seat of his trousers, trying to uncoil the underpants he has worn for the whole of the week. Oroteña knows this because, in one of her wilder excesses, she had offered to do his washing.

The thought of him wearing none at all re-awakened the clairvoyant in her.

Guiseppe drew the coffee to the edge of the table, inserted his finger in the loop and held the cup high.

'*Saludo*! Who shall go first?'

Oroteña places a hand on Maurice's arm to hold the visible, verbal tide at bay. Maurice's face turns pink with effort. His eyes search this way and that as if looking for somewhere to safely explode.

Oroteña lifts her touch. 'I think it should be Maurice.'

Maurice shudders, his face cooling, his eyes losing their so recent wildness, his handkerchief dabbing at his forehead.

'Thank God for that!' He sags theatrically into the chair and shakes his head.

'Seppy. We have been… we have *all* been friends for many years.'

Guiseppe nods sagely as Maurice draws a long breath to continue.

'And, having that as a background to our relationship, we have learned to notice when one of our friends is in trouble. Is this not so?'

Guiseppe continues to nod sagely. Oroteña places a hand on Maurice's arm again, but having marched to the golden beat of his dreams, Maurice is unstoppable.

'Many times… no… *so* many times… you have been the one to our rescue, Seppy. I remember the time of the dog in the street just outside… the one with the missing teeth…'

Oroteña taps on his arm but Maurice is in tidal flood like the river behind the café in Spring.

Guiseppe takes a strong breath and interrupts.

'I also remember the dog, Maurice. And the reason for the missing teeth.'

'Then there you are!' Maurice beams in appreciation. 'That's what friends do.'

'I took you to the Doctor, Maurice. That's all I did.'

'Ah yes, my friend. But why did you take me?'

'Because the dog's missing teeth were embedded in your leg bone, Maurice.'

'But that's what friends do, Seppy. That's what friends are for. You also took me to the Dentist after the Doctor refused to extract them.'

'Professional demarcation lines, Maurice. A modern disease that is rarely transgressed, but often regretted.'

'There, you see. You are a true friend.'

'So, Maurice. Which one of us is in trouble? Yourself?'

'No, Seppy… I…'

'Oroteña?'

Oroteña shakes her head, smiling at the assertion.

'I am constantly in trouble, Seppy. Accountants, taxmen, clients, this building falling down around my ears and my best friends and customers are two crotchety old farts who can't even talk sense. But that aside… no, it is not me.'

Guiseppe takes a look at the eager expressions on

the faces beside him.

'Then help me out here. I'm running out of options.'

Oroteña haunts her face with an expression of concern that is so fleeting Seppy is not convinced it was ever there.

'Seppy… We are here to help… you.'

*

Señor Rallentandó eases comfortably around in his seat.

'Señor Marino… of course I can write you a Will. But then it will have to be notarised and witnessed separately before it comes into force.'

'Can't I just say it, you just write it and I just sign it? You know, as they say, keep it simple?'

'Life is rarely simple, Señor, which is why you are here today.'

'To make it more complicated?'

'No, Señor. I would dispute that. In my professional opinion a Will and Testament requires couching in a form of language that another professional may interpret in the way that you originally meant it to be read.'

'And if that means *I* no longer understand it?'

'That is of little consequence. It matters only that the solicitor engaged by any subsequent beneficiary understands the intent of the language.'

'There was a time…' Guiseppe sighs and leans his back against the hard-railed chair, staring at the rows of books on the high shelves as if searching for a particular volume.

'…when the Church burned at the stake anyone with the temerity to print the Bible in plain language. So many secrets were hidden within their vestments, you see?'

'Señor… I am sure not…'

'No longer, it seems.' Guiseppe smiles across the desk at the solicitor. 'Now that Latin is no longer the weapon of choice amongst the professions, obscurantism has become the recourse of those who would protect their skill and art.'

'Señor Marino? What were you in your past life?'

'I carried fish.'

'What kind of fish?'

'The usual kind.'

'Not men?'

'No, Señor Rallentandó. I am no Saint, nor is my name Pedro and of that I am glad.'

'But you seem to me to be more than capable of…'

'Señor, when confronted by boxes of fish I could choose how many to carry, depending, of course, on the size of my breakfast that morning, the hours of my sleep and the willingness or otherwise of my arms. That is an easy calculation. It is much harder to contemplate the weight of mankind's wishes.'

The solicitor wipes his glasses clean to look more closely at Guiseppe.

'Forgive me, Señor, but I think you well-schooled. Is this the secret buried deep within your own vestments?'

Guiseppe leans forward in return. 'Only fish are schooled. They are learned solely in the art of swimming together.'

'And there is harm in this?'

'No harm, Señor, but that is how they end up in a box. And other than flesh, there is no weight in the box.'

'No weight of thought, then?'

'Señor Rallentandó, a fish is where thought goes to die.'

'And you have kept your thoughts alive, Señor Marino?'

'Certainly. What else is a man supposed to do when his life is spent carrying dead fish?'

'Returning to this thought of death, Señor Marino. In respect of your own, do you have a reason to suspect that it is impending?'

Guiseppe laughs out loud.

'I am seventy-eight years old, Señor. It has been impending for the last decade.'

'But is there any reason, apart from the legacy which you recently received to, forgive my expression, 'rush' into a simple Will?'

'Love. Señor Rallentandó. Simple... Pure... Love.'

The solicitor places his pen back in the desk holder and relaxes into his chair.

'Love is often Pure, Señor Marino, but never simple. Take it from a solicitor.'

'And if the Love is Pure, but the man is simple? Is that not another equation?'

'Then tell me about Love, Señor Marino. While I contemplate the benefits of Life outside the fish box.'

'Fish box indeed. When I was a young man my father took ship until, one day, the ship took him. My mother waited for him until days passed far beyond the stretch of her belief, then fell into an abyss far deeper than the one my father resides in… so far down she was unreachable. When she died the last thing I saw in her eyes was hope, that scourge of man that befalls him in his hour of last resort, but I was not alongside her in despair. From her abyss had shone a light that began to burn so brightly there were days that I could no longer see clearly. A man needs shadows you know? He needs them so that he can sort through the light and shade of his life in order to make sense of it and there were times that my sister Nella's light was all I could see. There was no shade. Just tiny, newborn Nella. And the responsibility for her preservation made it impossible for me to see beyond that. I allowed it to consume me despite the weight it brought, that vision allowing me to tread lightly upon the water of my own life, feeling it wash around my feet while my sole intent was to keep her above it. At times I looked down to see my reflection and there wasn't one and yet in those days I could carry twenty boxes of fish with little effort and my arms were as strong as you'd expect, but as she grew my duty to Nella gradually weighed upon me so heavily that it weakened me until I felt myself sinking. Stealthily, the water rose up to my knees, my thighs, my waist until I was sure the waves had the power to devour me… and then what would happen to Nella, Señor? That I did not know.'

'What did happen to Nella?'

'She brought me a Hero, Señor. In all of the truest sense of the word. A Hero who took the weight of Nella from my shoulders and, in that moment, I thought him a God.'

'How did he do that?'

'He married her, Señor.'

'Surely a cause for Joy, Guiseppe.'

'In doing so, Señor, he replaced the weight of Nella with another.'

'How could he do that?'

'With the weight of Nella lifted from my shoulders I rose again out of the waters of life. Below my feet they calmed until I could see my own reflection.'

Señor Rallentandó leans forward expectantly.

'And what did it show?'

'It showed that I was in love with him, too.'

'And now you are ready to put down that burden?'

'No, Señor. He does not know and I can never tell him. Maybe not even with my dying breath. I cannot give back the burden he unwittingly placed upon me. I love him far too much for that.'

*

'Where is he today, Maurice?'

Oroteña replaces the third cup beneath the counter. Not really understanding the impulse, she draws it forward to the edge of the shelf.

'He is at the solicitors again. Good job he has an inheritance. Service like that can be a money-sponge.'

'What's he doing this time?'

'I can't remember. He said it was important.'

'Then how can you forget?'

'It's easy. Like you forgot to bring my coffee.'

'Sorry, Maurice.'

Oroteña turns around and stares hard into each corner of the room.

Maurîce makes a pretence of lifting a cup.

'Why are you staring at the walls, Oroteña. Aren't you sick of the sight after all these years?'

'Sometimes I like to look at what's mine, Maurîce. Sometimes I wish the walls were not there and sometimes I'm glad they are. Sometimes I need that reassurance.'

'You need reassurance, Oroteña? You're the most self-sufficient woman I ever came across.'

'Sometimes I think I need a man, Maurîce.'

'Why's that. Think he'll help you remember my coffee?'

'A real man might have helped me remember my life, Maurîce, a life we shared together. Maybe just moments. Chicken-pecks in the sand, like those photographs I see on laptop screens that waft in and out whenever they open and close their machines. A real man might even have been a memory in himself.'

'I once was.'

'You was once what, Maurîce?'

'I was once a man.'

'When was that?'

'I'm not sure. Perhaps it's just a memory.'

'A false one would be better than none at all.'

'A false man?'

'No, Maurîce. A false memory of one. It might have seemed more real than daydreams. There are days when I could've been a mother, a wife, then a grandmother the like of which you would not believe.'

'When was that, Oroteña?'

'Oh… most days, Maurîce. Sometime between siesta and tequila o'clock.'

'What happened to your husband, Oroteña. You never said.'

'Which one?'

'I don't know. How many have you had?'

'As many as there were stars in the Yankee pictures at the Saturday Matinee.'

'I meant a real one.'

'What's a real one, Maurice? Are you a real one?'

'I was a real one.'

'Ah, yes. Nella. And now what are you?'

'Ashamed.'

'Of what do you need to be ashamed, Maurice? You stood by that girl through everything. You held her hand wherever you went. Like two schoolchildren.'

'Oroteña? Is it wrong to love twice?'

'Once would have been a fine thing, Maurice. I might then know what you are talking about.'

'Fetch my coffee. Then I'll tell you.'

*

'Señor Marino. Now you have had time to reflect on the terms of your Will, have you reconsidered them at all?'

'I have, Señor. But only insofar as I wish to expand upon my reasons for them.'

'You wish to leave a letter alongside your Will?'

'No. I intend to embody the terms into the Will itself. If that is permitted under law?'

'Certainly… Guiseppe… There is no law against this but instigation can become a problem. There may also be certain challenges… in terms of verification that your wishes have been followed.'

'And how much will that cost?'

Señor Rallentandó stares in thought for a moment, chin cupped by his palm. He then picks up a pencil and behind a shielding hand draws a quick caricature of his dog on his notepad. Considering it critically, he then makes an adjustment to the ears. That was so much better he couldn't help but smile. He looks up into Guiseppe's waiting face.

'Another two point five percent.'

'Done.'

The solicitor taps the side of a small hand-sized machine between them on the desk. The tiny screen leaps into electrical life.

'Then, Señor Marino, begin your dictation.'

Guiseppe coughs loudly and watches the little needle on the machine rocket back and forth against an etched scale.

'Harum… Humph…' He stops, fascinated by the action engendered by… well, not even words.

'Señor Marino… Guiseppe… you may begin.'

*

Oroteña returns to the table with two fresh coffees and sets them down. Maurice drinks his abruptly, as if he were taking poison and leaving no time for second thoughts or regret. He shudders as he puts down the cup. Poison might be easier than honesty, some days. Days like this one, in which his past thoughts and wishes gather around him like a cloak under which his regrets and recriminations are hidden.

An honest response to Oroteña's question, at his age, as well as being overdue, was certain to rip that cloak right off.

He begins by taking a deep breath.

'Nella and I had been married for around two years when a sudden fate descended on me, though it was none of my making. I was reading Economics at University so, I suppose, any good Communista might suggest that I was culpable just by sheer dint of my supposed intelligence. I never wanted to go there. I never even wanted to study Economics. It's pointless, you either have money or you don't have money. Who needs someone so over-educated that they can tell you why? Does that fill your belly? No. It only fills theirs. It seems the new government shared my view on the subject. They closed down the course and shortly after they closed down the entire University. Since when do Communistas want anyone around who is intelligent enough to shine a light on their economic debacle?'

'That should have saved you money. University fees were expensive back then.'

'Not for me, Oroteña. My father was entirely suspicious of me as a young man. He studied my friends and companions, none of whom he approved, and he made me sign an agreement that if I married Nella he would pay the fees and make me an allowance so that we could manage, as he remarked himself, very carefully, until I had established my place in our country's Great Economic Future, as he called it. The Communistas had other ideas. I went to work for him after they closed the University and soon after that they shut down our factory because my father refused to make bullets for them. 'People don't need gew-gaws and trinkets in order to live,' they said. 'What about the people who make and sell them,' I asked. Their answer was fifty-six days in solitary.'

Oroteña pushes back her chair, liberating her belly-pan from the hard rim of the table and taking a deep breath.

'I was still a child in those days, Maurice. Not young, but still a child. I got by because people dismissed me. I was so fat that, when the soldiers came through like the Lords they imagined themselves to be, I was overlooked. That was how I survived. I suppose that is how I have always survived… and how I will continue to, by all reckoning.'

'You didn't build fat, Oroteña. You built a wall. No-one ever try to climb over it?'

'Not a one, Maurice.'

'They never knew you.'

'They couldn't know me, Maurice. The wall was too high.'

'Still?'

Oroteña spreads her arms out wide and the flesh hangs beneath them in waves. Characteristically folding them again, her breasts descend to rest on her prodigious stomach.

'What do you see, Maurice?'

Maurice thinks for a moment.

'A woman who probably knows me better than I do.'

'And behind the wall?'

'For that I would need the incentive to build a ladder.'

'Perhaps you should have been a carpenter.'

'I could have been many things. When my economic fate befell me I asked Seppy to get me a job with him at the Fish Market. Anything to be able to meet my commitment to Nella and my father.'

'Then why didn't you?'

'I tried. I knew it wouldn't be easy but my arms had 'pen' muscles, not ones of iron like Seppy. The day I asked him he had a strange look in his eye. He said that there were no jobs available but I knew that wasn't true. He could have persuaded them, but he wouldn't. For days after he continued to look at me in such a strange fashion that I began to think there was something wrong with me. Something only others could see. I searched in the mirror. I had my photograph taken on the Promenade. Several times.'

'Did you ever find it, Maurice?'

'Yes, I did. One Natividad he bought himself a Box Brownie camera and wanted to try it out. I posed with my arm as far as I could around Nella. She was pregnant then.'

'Oh, Maurice. I didn't know you had a child.'

'I don't. I... we didn't. The foetus stalled like the others that came after it. But at this time she was in full bloom and we wanted a picture of it.'

'Do you still have it?'

'Maybe... somewhere. I think it's behind another one in a frame. It hurts to look at it.'

'I can imagine. Poor Nella.'

'Poor Nella indeed, but that wasn't the hurt.'

'Then what could have hurt you so much more than that?'

'When Seppy was taking the picture he was looking

down into the camera to frame the shot but then kept looking up to make sure we were smiling and still. What I recognised then was the look in his eye. He seemed to hesitate. I think he sensed what I had seen in that moment. Within another second he had pressed a shutter on forever.'

'What was it that you saw, Maurice? Was he jealous of you with Nella? I know they were close. She used to tell me that it sometimes worried her.'

'That is true, Oroteña. But he wasn't jealous of me. He was jealous of Nella. Because the look in his eye said he also was in love with me.'

'This happens, Maurice. It is not a thing to be ashamed of. It is good that other people love and admire you. If only I…'

'That is not the whole of it, Oroteña. One week later when the photograph was developed he brought us a copy.

'That is a kindness, Maurice. Not a thing out of love.'

'Yes, but when he brought the picture I looked closely at it, out of habit almost, and that's when I discovered it.'

'And what was it?'

'I had the same look in mine.'

*

'How shall I start?'

'That is entirely up to you, Señor Marino… Guiseppe. Pick a moment.'

'There are too many, and sometimes they are lost in

the fog of time.'

'This is a time for clarity, Guiseppe. You cannot leave behind you a mist of intent. It must be claro for all to see and for me to act upon. What is your dearest wish?'

'Can you take me back in time?'

'Unfortunately not, but I can remind you that all that is past is now informing your present and illuminating your forward path. Take the light. It will show you the way.'

'The path... the light... It meanders around three lonely people who, despite it's brilliance, cannot clearly see each other. How can I make that claro?'

'Guiseppe, this is your opportunity to make a change, to control and direct that light to ensure that things become claro. But remember that when dealing with people, we can only illuminate our wishes for them, we cannot make them take a path they do not wish for themselves.'

Guiseppe taps the desk with his fingers, sending the little needle rocketing again. He watches it with amusement, then taps the desk again.

'Señor Rallentandó, perhaps people do not understand those things we describe as 'being in their best interests' until they have experienced them for themselves.'

'Are we speaking coercion, here Guiseppe?'

'I think we are, Señor.'

'Then that is a language I understand. Who, what, why and how? Is there 'a game afoot'?'

'If so, it is a simple one, Señor, with one proviso.'

'May I remind you we are still recording?'

Guiseppe taps the table again and the needle responds in the way he hopes that one day his Will might.

'I… Guiseppe Marino… being of somewhat sound mind… leave this, my Last Will and Testament, as follows;

I leave the whole of the residue of my Estate to be shared equally between Oroteña Obregas and Maurîce Gonzalez, subject to the following Proviso;

That within two weeks of my demise they shall be married and live together for the rest of their lives.

If that Proviso fails, my Estate shall be dispersed amongst various local charities.'

'That is an unusual Proviso, Guiseppe. How do you think they will react to it?'

'I think that Maurîce will take a chance that poverty has denied him all his life and Oroteña will seize the opportunity to end the emotional drought in which she was marooned at childhood.'

'And your hope in all this, Guiseppe?'

'That her flesh engulfs him in the way that my love should have done all these years, had I but dared to bring a voice to it.'

'She has that capacity, Guiseppe?'

'Enough to drown him, Señor.'

*

'Oroteña! Coffee for three!'

Maurîce reaches across the table to steady Seppy's waving arm. 'Hey, Seppy. You late for something? You are never in a rush. You're always the last down for breakfast.'

Oroteña sways towards them with three coffees and sets them carefully, brushing aside the arm Maurîce has left across the table.

'I can only move so fast, Seppy. Here's your coffee. I'll be back in a minute. The guy with the laptop…'

Seppy grabs her apron and holds her to the table.

'Forget Señor Wi-Fi for a minute. Sit down.'

Oroteña scrunches her behind between the arms of the aluminium chair.

'Valé! I am here now. What is the rush?'

'There is no rush, but we have plans to make and I need your help.'

Maurîce sits up to the table. 'We have plans to make?'

'Yes. I can't do this without you two and an airplane.'

'Do what, Seppy?'

'Use up the remaining three hundred and thirty-eight thousand, seven hundred and fifty Airmiles that my Uncle won in a Lottery.'

*

Guiseppe leans across Maurîce's lap to stare out of the window. On his left, Oroteña is crammed into the tiny aisle seat. The stewardess has lifted the folding arms between them and Oroteña spills over into his space, pushing him further into Maurîce who, having rushed on board to grab the window seat, now has nowhere to go.

'Seppy? Can you sit up a little?'

Guiseppe ignores him to keep staring through the

window at the blue rim of the world. He reaches for both their hands and grips them tightly, sitting up in the seat as far as he is able without shifting his gaze from the window.

Outside, twin propellers shear the clear air into ribbons of fleece while the sunlit wing flashes a polished aluminum glare back into his eyes. Above him, the blue gradually fades to black where, although dim, he knows the stars will soon blossom with their forever light… and he wonders which one is Nella.

Maurice trembles beside him against the airplane wall.

'Seppy! Take that silly grin off your face. Aren't you afraid at your age to be this close to Heaven and surrounded by less than nothing at all?'

Guiseppe lowers his head slowly and gracefully until it rests on Maurice's shoulder.

'Not at all, Maurice… I've never been nearer my God than this.'

If you have enjoyed NEARER MY GOD, then take a look on AMAZON for the first two chronicles of my MEKANISMO trilogy. World-spanning over 2000 years, framed by historical fact and written under my byline of 'William Allerton', this is a story of great love, deception and emotions twisted by the pursuit of the Antikythera Device in which strong, intense females lead the narrative.

My other novels and short stories are written under the more familiar name of 'Bill Allerton' and are all available and in print;

'The Fox & The Fish' (A darkly comic novel)
'Magpie' (Slides from humour into violent darkness)
'Mekanismo 1' Keepers of The Bell (William Allerton)
'Mekanismo 2' Argo Navis (William Allerton)
'Mekanismo 3' Ophiuchus Rising (In preparation)
'Firelight on Dark Water' (Short Fiction)
'A Day for Tigers' (Short 'Old Style' Science Fiction)
'Foxes, Frogs & Rice Pudding' (Stories for Children)
'Sir Tingly & The Time Mouse' (Stories for Children)

For more information about Cybermouse Books and our Authors, please visit our website @:

www.cybermouse.co.uk

where you will find downloadable Free Excerpts from our current books and an ability to buy them directly from us at a discount with FREE POSTAGE in the UK.

To hear more of our output, visit URBAN TIGER RADIO on Soundcloud via this link:

https://soundcloud.com/rbanigeradio

or look for us on your own podcast player, select 'follow' or 'subscribe' (It won't cost you anything!) and have a free listen to all our amazing podcasts of incredibly talented writers and performers you will never hear anywhere else.

www.ingramcontent.com/pod-product-compliance
Lightning Source LLC
Chambersburg PA
CBHW042301030526
44119CB00066B/843